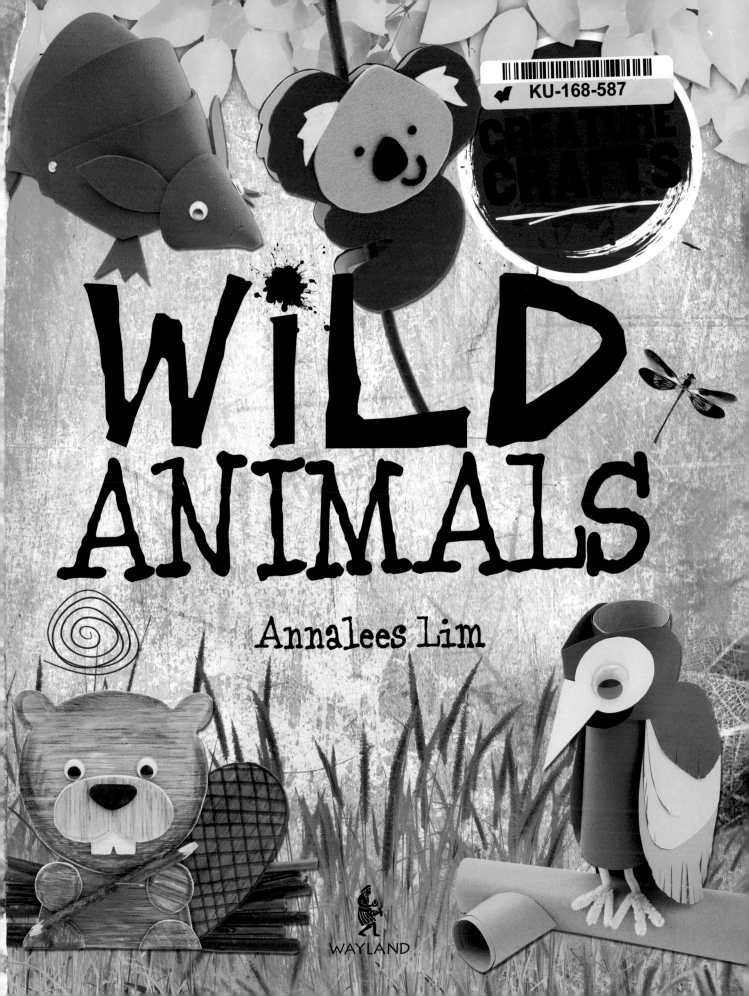

CREATURE CRAFTS

WILD ANIMALS

Annalees Lim

WAYLAND

CONTENTS

Welcome to the world of
wild animals!

Which animals have you seen in the wild before? Would you like to make some of your own and find out loads of fun facts about them along the way? Then this book is for you!

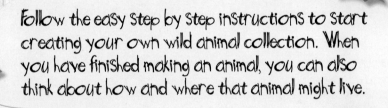

Follow the easy step by step instructions to start creating your own wild animal collection. When you have finished making an animal, you can also think about how and where that animal might live.

A lot of the projects use paint and PVA glue. Always cover surfaces with a piece of plastic or layers of old newspaper. Whenever you can, leave the project to dry before moving on to the next step. This avoids things getting stuck to each other or paint smudging.

So, do you have your craft tools at the ready? Then get set to make your crafty creatures and discover what makes each of them so special!

You can even follow QR codes to watch videos of how some of the crafts are made!

FLOATING HIPPO

You will need:
Small water bottle
Dark blue, white, black and light blue foam
Craft glue
Scissors

Optional:
Masking tape

Hippos live in hot areas. They spend a lot of time in water to keep cool. Once you have made your hippo, try floating it in water, too!

1

Screw the lid tightly onto the water bottle. Wrap the whole bottle in light blue foam and stick in place with the craft glue. You might need to use some masking tape to hold the foam in place until it dries.

2

Cut out shapes from the light blue foam: a 'B' shape for your hippo's nose, a quarter of a circle (with the tip trimmed off), 2 ears and a tail.

Stick the 'B' shape onto the bottle lid. Bend the quarter circle around the neck of the bottle to make the hippo's face.

Stick the rest of the blue pieces onto the bottle using the craft glue. Leave to dry.

Make some eyes from the black and the white foam, and some inner ears and nostrils from the dark blue foam. Stick them in place with craft glue.

HIPPO FACT
Did you know that the hippo is one of the most dangerous animals in the world? It has huge teeth and powerful jaws.

BUG-EYED FROG

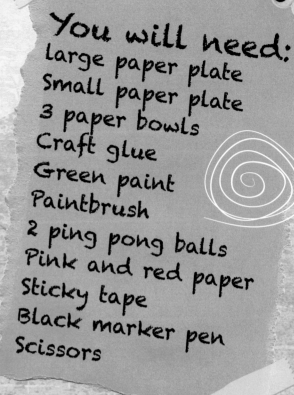

Frogs have big, round eyes that help them to see in many directions at once. Use ping pong balls to make your frog's eyes enormous!

1

Paint the paper plates and bowls green and leave them to dry. Draw some black dots onto 2 ping pong balls to make eyes.

2

Cut an equally sized piece off the side of 2 bowls. Stick them together to make your frog's body.

3

Cut the large paper plate into quarters, then cut the rim off each piece. These will form your frog's legs. Cut the centre pieces to make 4 feet.

4

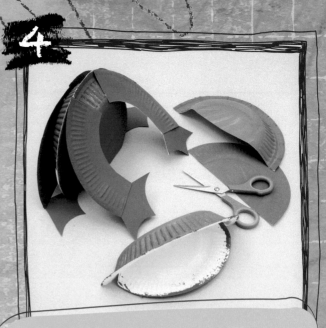

Glue the feet to the legs, and all 4 legs to your frog's body. Cut out a circle from pink paper. Make sure it's the size of a bowl. Cut a bowl and the small plate in half. Glue half of each to the pink circle to form the frog's head.

5

Cut out a tongue shape from red paper and stick it to the mouth. Use sticky tape to attach the eyes to the top of the head and then the head to the body.

FROG FACT
Young frogs are called tadpoles. They are black and have a long tail.

BALSA BEAVER

You will need:
Scrap card
Thin balsa wood
    sheets
Scissors
Craft glue
Googly eyes
Black felt tip pen
Coloured crayons
Twigs

Beavers have long, sharp teeth that they use to cut through wood. They use the wood to build homes, called lodges.

1

Draw the shapes for your beaver's body parts onto scrap card. Cut out all the shapes.

2

Using the card shapes as templates, draw your beaver's body parts onto the balsa wood. Cut them out with the scissors. You might need an adult to help you with the cutting.

3

Use crayons to colour in the body parts. You can use a felt tip pen to add a criss-cross pattern to the tail.

4

Glue all the body parts together to make your beaver. Glue on some googly eyes.

5

Glue the twigs to the back of your beaver to help him stand up. You can even place one twig in his paws!

BEAVER FACT
Beavers build huge dams made of twigs, mud and branches. Some are up to 4 metres high!

CROC CARD

Crocodiles have up to 80 teeth! You don't have to make all 80 for this crafty croc, but make sure they are all sharp and white.

You will need:
2 x A4 green card
1 x A4 blue paper
White paper
Scissors
Glue stick
Black marker pen
Ruler

1

Fold one piece of green card in half, lengthways, and cut lots of slits along the fold. Start with 2 that 3cm apart. Make sure the slits in the middle are longer than those at the ends.

2

Open the card and pop out the slitted sections. These will form your crocodile.

3

Cut a triangle shape out of the longest section to make the mouth. Using some green card, cut out a 'B' shape that is as wide as your croc's head.

4

Stick the 'B' shape to the croc's head. Cut out two rows of sharp teeth from white paper. Stick them to the inside of the mouth. Cut out eyes, feet, nostrils and a tail.

5

Stick all the body parts on, apart from the feet. Cut a shape out of blue paper to fit around your croc. Glue it to the card. Add the croc's feet and draw plants around it.

CROCODILE FACT
Did you know that crocodiles hold their mouths open in hot weather to help them cool down?

Watch this video of how to make your croc card!

11

GIRAFFE PUPPET

The pattern on each giraffe is unique – no two giraffes look the same. Why not create a special pattern for your giraffe!

You will need:
5 toilet roll tubes
Yellow and brown paper
Googly eyes
Glue stick
String
Stapler
30cm long wooden dowelling
Scissors
Ruler
Sticky tape

1

Cut 3 toilet roll tubes in half and keep the other 2 whole. Cover all tubes in yellow paper. Decorate all but one short tube with patches of brown paper, stuck down with the glue stick.

2

Tie 4 pieces of string along the wooden dowelling. The pieces should each be 30 cm long. Feed the first string through the short yellow tube and staple in place.

3

Thread 2 long tubes onto the same string and staple them, too. Tie the ends of the first and the last string on the dowelling together.

4

Thread 2 short tubes onto the ends of both middle strings to make the legs. Staple them in place. Use sticky tape to fix the strings to the body of your giraffe.

5

Cut into the head to make a mouth and cut some ears and a tail out of yellow card. Use strips of brown paper to make the mane, the tail end and the hooves. Glue on the eyes.

GIRAFFE FACT
Giraffes are the tallest animals in the world. They are 3 times as tall as an adult human!

CLIMBING KOALA

You will need:
Two clothes pegs
Grey card
Dark grey, light grey, white and black felt
Fabric glue
Scissors
Pencil

Koalas live in eucalyptus trees in Australia. Craft your koala so that it can hang from plants in your home!

1

Draw a koala shape onto grey card, making sure that it is wider than the length of a peg. Cut it out and then draw around it to make a second koala shape.

2

Stick both koala shapes onto the dark grey felt and cut them out.

3

Cut out the shape of the koala's face from light grey felt. Stick it onto one of the koala shapes.

4

Cut out 2 ear tufts from white felt and eyes, a nose and a mouth from black felt. Stick them all on the koala's face.

5

Sandwich the pegs in between both koala shapes. Fix the pegs in place with fabric glue.

KOALA FACT
Did you know that koalas aren't bears? They are related to wombats and kangaroos.

POM-POM PANDA

You will need:
Small and large
pom-poms in
black and
in white
Fabric glue
Googly eyes
Green pipe cleaners
Florist oasis
Black felt
Scissors

There are fewer than 2,000 pandas left in the wild. Make your own cuddly panda and keep it in a bamboo forest.

1

Glue 2 white pom-poms to each other. Then glue a small white pom-pom to one of the larger ones.

2

Glue 6 small black pom-poms onto the white body to make the ears, arms and legs of your panda.

3

Cut shapes out of the black felt for the eyes and nose. Glue them to the head and then glue on googly eyes.

4

Cut 5 pipe cleaners in half. Cut 5 others into 10 pieces each. Wrap the small pieces around the longer ones to make bamboo shoots.

5

Press all but one of the bamboo plants into the florist oasis. Set the panda in the scene. Place the last bamboo plant in your panda's paws.

PANDA FACT
In the wild, pandas only eat bamboo shoots.

PRETTY PARROT

You will need:
Red, yellow, blue and green card
Black and white paper
Yellow pipe cleaners
Glue stick
Scissors
Googly eyes
Kitchen roll tube
Optional:
Brown card

These brightly coloured birds live in warm parts of the world. Follow the steps to make a scarlet macaw with colourful wings!

1

Bend one end of 2 pipe cleaners. Twist a shorter length of pipe cleaner to each of them to form claws.

2

Roll a large piece of red card around a kitchen roll tube. Stick it in place with glue.

3

Cut wing shapes in different sizes from blue, green, yellow and red card. Cut slits into the edges. Cut 3 tail feather shapes from red card.

4

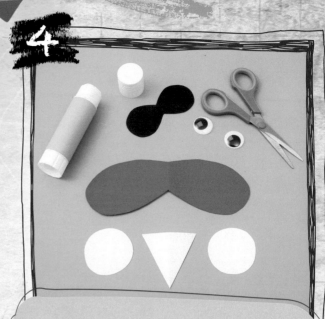

Cut a shape for the face from red card. Use white paper to make the beak and two circles to hold the eyes. Cut out a black shape that looks like an '8'.

5

Glue all the shapes together, and stick on googly eyes. Glue the pipe cleaners to the inside of your parrot's body. You can make a branch for it to sit on by rolling up some brown card.

PARROT FACT
Macaws have very powerful beaks that can crack nut shells!

ARMOURED ARMADILLO

The armadillo is the only animal to have plates of 'armour' on its body! Some can even roll up into a ball to protect themselves.

1

Cut 5 brown strips of foam that measure 7cm x 20cm.

2

Arrange all the strips into a fan shape. Fix them together using a paper fastener.

3

Bend all the strips and fix them together on the other side using another paper fastener. Trim the corners of the strips.

4

Cut out 4 feet, 2 ears, a tail and a semicircle to form your armadillo's head.

ARMADILLO FACT
The word 'armadillo' is Spanish for 'little armoured one'!

5

Fold the semicircle to form a cone shape. Glue all the shapes onto your armadillo and add googly eyes. You may need to use masking tape to hold everything in place until the glue has dried.

Watch this video of how to make your armadillo!

FEATHERY OSTRICH

Ostriches are the largest birds in the world! They live in small groups, called herds. Why not make your own crafty ostrich herd!

1

Stack 3 wooden spoons, with the head of the middle one higher than the others. Wrap black electrical tape around the centre of the stack, and white electrical tape around the rest of the spoons.

2

Form 2 feet out of modelling clay, making sure they are quite thick.

3

Press the two handles into the modelling clay feet to make your ostrich stand up.

4

Stick lots of black feathers onto the body to make your ostrich's wings.

5

Cut and fold a beak from pink paper. Stick it onto the face using the fabric glue. Stick on googly eyes.

OSTRICH FACT

An ostrich's legs are very powerful. When they run, their strides can be 5 metres long!

GLOSSARY

bamboo shoot	the young part of a bamboo plant that has just sprouted
dam	a mound of twigs, mud and leaves that beavers build across rivers
puppet	a kind of doll that has strings attached to it; you can move the doll by pulling the strings
unique	when something is one of a kind, not like anything else

INDEX

First published in 2015 by Wayland

Copyright © Wayland 2015

Wayland
338 Euston Road
London NW1 3BH

Wayland Australia
Level 17/207 Kent Street
Sydney NSW 2000

All rights reserved.

Wayland, part of Hachette Children's Group and published by Hodder and Stoughton Limited

www.hachette.co.uk

Series editor: Julia Adams
Craft photography: Simon Pask, N1 Studios
Additional images: Shutterstock

ISBN: 9780750284493
ebook ISBN: 9780750293792

Printed in China

The QR codes included in this book were valid at the time of going to press. However, because of the nature of the Internet, it is possible that addresses may have changed, or sites may have changed or closed down, since publication.

Get your paws on all the books in the Creature Crafts series!

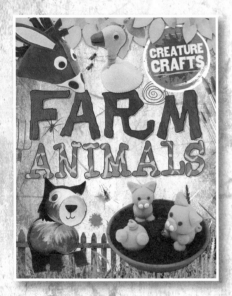

978 0 7502 8448 6

978 0 7502 8447 9

978 0 7502 9543 7

978 0 7502 8446 2

978 0 7502 8449 3

978 0 7502 9544 4